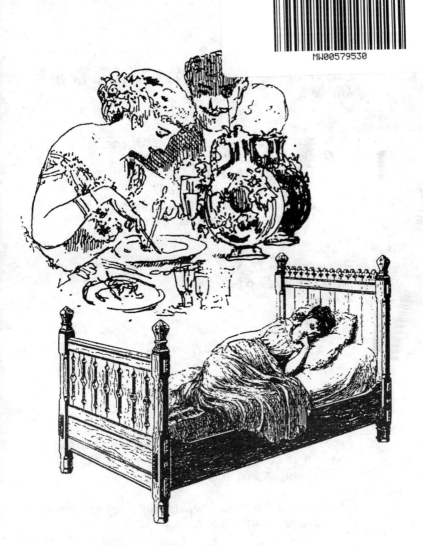

Delightful Dreams of Dixie Dinners

Entrees, Accompaniments, and Desserts
PLUS
Entertaining Recollections

Patricia B. Mitchell

Published 1992 by the author at Mitchells, P. O. Box 429, Chatham, VA 24531.
Telephone: 434-432-0595
Book Sales: 800-967-2867
E-mail: answers@foodhistory.com
Website: www.foodhistory.com

Printed in the U. S. A.
ISBN 0-925117-63-3

Sixth Printing, July 2006

- *Illustrations* -

Front Cover - figures by Charles Dana Gibson in a collage of images from Dover Publications, Inc., New York.

Inside Title Page - a collage of images from Dover Publications, Inc.

Inside Back Cover - portrait of the author by David L. Mitchell.

Back Cover - "Celestial Natchez," by Henry H. Mitchell, a posterized print depicting Venus and the Moon over the Mississippi River, as seen from "Under the Hill" at Natchez on the evening of July 13, 1991 (see page 2).

Table of Contents

A Feel of Dreams

This book was originally entitled **Delightful Nights of Dixie Dinners**, *but it was suggested to me that it would be better to call it* **Delightful Dreams of Dixie Dinners**. *I like the new name better because it contains more alliteration. (Remember Rudyard Kipling's "great, grey-green, greasy Limpopo River?") And because dreams sound, well,* **dreamy**. *And the South and things Southern are the stuff dreams are made of. I personally love the stereotypical Southland images — Spanish moss, magnolia blossoms, white-columned antebellum mansions, pert and flirty misses, dashing gentlemen, dark and mysterious gumbo, drippy-sweet watermelon slices, Holy Ghost revivals, and riverbank baptisms, honeysuckle-scented nights and throbbing soul music, "easy living, rich daddies, good-looking mammas, and other good gifts from God" — it's all true, and it's all here. Come on down South and see and taste and enjoy! This book will set you dreaming.*

Young Bride's Shrimp Creole

Cooking in Biloxi, Mississippi was a challenge. (*Eating* in Biloxi was a marvelous education about, and induction into, the world of Gulf Coast and Louisiana-style cuisine!) I'll tell you why cooking was difficult. — Henry was assigned to Keesler Air Force Base just after Hurricane Camille had leveled much of Biloxi (back in '69). We were blessed to find an intact house to rent. The stove, though, was an old gas model. (I had never cooked with gas before.) Most chefs, as you know, prefer gas stoves because the temperature can be regulated more precisely . . . . I was inexperienced, though, and the stove temperamental. Immediately after the hurricane, utilities were non-functioning, and the gas off, of course. Along with the flooding, rain, wind, roof damage, and salt spray from the ocean came extraordinarily high humidity. Resulting corrosion had caused the gas jets on my range to often not light at all, to flicker, flare up and down unpredictably, and in general act quite contrary. It was an *interesting* experience to cook a meal (especially in a hurry). Nevertheless, we loved Biloxi — the people, the food, the climate. (Recent trips there demonstrate that food in Biloxi is still tantalizing.)

One great advantage of living in Biloxi was the fact that we could buy fresh shrimp right off the boat in the Back Bay. The first Shrimp Creole I happened to learn to prepare was according to the following recipe. (The chili powder is a Texas touch, but that's what was called for.) When I was mastering this easy dish, we bought fresh shrimp for 39¢ a pound!

* * *

2 tbsp. vegetable oil
1 large onion, chopped
1 sm. green (bell) pepper, chopped
4 stalks celery, sliced
1 tbsp. chili powder
Salt to taste
2 c. tomatoes (fresh or canned, cut up)
1 sm. can tomato sauce
1/2 c. water
2 lb. raw cleaned shrimp
Cooked rice

Sauté the vegetables in the oil until the onion becomes translucent. Add the remaining ingredients except for the shrimp. Simmer the mixture 30 minutes in a covered pot. Stir occasionally. Add shrimp. Cook about 10 minutes or until the shrimp is just firm. Serve over cooked rice.

Natchez Sky Watch

One of the most breathtaking sights I have ever seen is the Natchez, Mississippi, bridge, viewed at night from Natchez-Under-the-Hill, a section of town beside the river. When a crescent moon and Venus glisten over the lights of the bridge a cosmically exquisite composition is created.

Perhaps the best way to prepare oneself for viewing this or some other similar late-evening celestial phenomenon is to spend a couple of hours in a restaurant, forking in some fresh seafood, or eating in the home of friends, or dining with friends in a favorite eatery. With Jimmie and Honey Gross of Woodville, Mississippi, we ate a supper of cornbread and coleslaw (served as a separate first course — a local habit in Natchez, I understand) and then fried (or broiled) catfish and fried or baked potatoes. When we eventually got back to Woodville, Honey fed us again!

Cornbread

1/2 tsp. salt
1/2 tsp. soda
1/2 tsp. baking powder
2 tbsp. oil or bacon drippings
1 egg, well-beaten
1/2 c. flour
1 c. buttermilk
1 c. plus 2 tbsp. cornmeal, sifted

Beat all ingredients together, beating well. Heat greased iron skillet until hot enough to sizzle. Bake 425° F. for 20 minutes or until brown.

For *corn sticks*, fill irons to 1/2 full. Bake at 450° F. for 10 minutes or until brown.

Note: The secret of good cornbread is beating well and using hot irons.

- recipe courtesy Teague's Mill, Gatlinburg, TN

Hush Puppies

1 c. cornmeal, sifted
1/2 c. flour

1 tsp. salt
2 tsp. baking powder
1 egg, well-beaten
3/4 - 1 c. milk
Pinch of sugar
1 small onion, chopped
1 tbsp. melted shortening

Sift the first four ingredients together. Add egg, milk, and onion. Add shortening. Mix thoroughly. Drop from a tablespoon (1/2 full) into deep hot fat, dipping spoon in cold water each time. Fry until golden brown.

- recipe courtesy Teague's Mill, Gatlinburg, TN

Creamy Coleslaw

6 c. finely-shredded green cabbage
1/3 c. chopped onion
1/3 c. chopped cucumber
1 c. shredded carrots

Prepare Creamy Dressing; toss with remaining ingredients.

Creamy Dressing:

2/3 c. mayonnaise or salad dressing
2 tbsp. sugar
2 tbsp. vinegar
1 tbsp. milk
1/2 tsp. salt
1/8 tsp. paprika

Mix all ingredients, refrigerate 1 hour before mixing with cabbage mixture. (Makes about 1 cup dressing.)

- recipe by Kitty Doss

Pistachio Nut Cake

Honey calls a nice present a "happy," as in "Bille Faye brought me a happy, a new cookbook." Here is Honey's "happy" cake.

* * *

1 white cake mix
1 c. vegetable oil
1 c. club soda
3 eggs
1 pkg. instant pistachio pudding mix
1 c. chopped nuts

Mix all ingredients. Bake at 350° F. until the cake springs back when touched.

Frosting:

1 1/4 c. milk
1 box pistachio pudding
8 oz. Cool Whip

Beat milk and pudding until thick. Fold in Cool Whip.

- by Honey Gross, from Woodville Red Recipes, published 1987 by Cookbook Publishers, Inc., Olathe, KS, for the Tabithas of Woodville, MS, p. 168.

Chocolate Ice Cream

5 eggs
2 c. sugar
1 tsp. vanilla
3 (13-oz.) cans evaporated milk
1 (16-oz.) can chocolate syrup
Milk

Beat eggs until light and fluffy; stir in sugar, vanilla, evaporated milk, and chocolate syrup. Pour into freezer can of a 1-gallon hand-type or electric freezer. Fill to within 3 inches of the top of the can with milk. Freeze according to instructions of the freezer manufacturer. Yield: about 1 gallon.

Microwave Bread Pudding with Rum Sauce

3 c. bread cubes (about 5 slices)
1 c. sugar
1 1/2 c. evaporated milk
3 eggs, slightly beaten
1 tsp. vanilla
1/8 tsp. salt
1/2 tsp. cinnamon
1/3 c. raisins
1/4 c. margarine, melted (1 1/2 minutes)

In a two-quart batter bowl, combine bread cubes and milk. Let stand 10 minutes. Stir in remaining ingredients; stir well. Pour in 8-inch glass ring mold or (deep sides) 1 quart casserole. Place on inverted glass pie plate or bottom rack position. Microwave at 70% power for 10 to 12 minutes, or until knife inserted near center comes out clean. Let stand 5 minutes. Serves 6.

Rum Sauce for Bread Pudding:

1/2 c. sugar
2 tbsp. cornstarch
1/2 tsp. cinnamon
1 c. evaporated milk
3 tbsp. margarine
1 1/2 tbsp. dark rum

In 1 1/2 or 2 quart casserole, combine sugar, cornstarch and cinnamon; blend well. Stir in milk; stir well. Microwave at 100% power for 4 to 4 1/2 minutes, or until thickened. Stir halfway through cooking. Stir in margarine until melted. Add rum; stir well to blend. Makes about 1 1/2 cups.

Tip: May use rum flavoring.

- by Honey Gross, from Woodville Red Recipes, p. 208.

Charleston Chicken Marengo

When we plan a trip, "Yours truly" actually plans a *tasting journey!* I inquire of Henry where we will likely be at such and such a meal, and then find out about a good restaurant in that location. (You can imagine what a "gourmet map" France and Louisiana represent to me!)

A few summers ago our family and my mother traveled by car to Disney World, Kennedy Space Center, etc., in Florida. On the way down we stayed in Savannah one night and enjoyed excellent seafood at Tassey's Pier Restaurant in Thunderhead. Henry found an itty-bitty pearl in his oysters-on-the-half-shell there! En route home we stayed in Charleston, and ate at the French Quarter Restaurant of the Lodge Alley Inn. We were privileged to dine on Chicken Marengo as prepared by Ward Morgan, who was the executive chef at that time. Subsequently I wrote and requested the chef's recipe for that mouth-watering entree, and here it is for you to savor, too!

* * *

4 skinless breasts of chicken - 6 oz. each
1/4 c. clarified butter
1/4 c. peeled pearl onions
1 tsp. minced garlic
2 c. white wine
3 c. brown chicken stock
1 bay leaf
1 tsp. thyme
1/4 c. tomato paste

2 tbsp. butter
3 tbsp. flour
1/2 c. baby mushroom caps
1/4 c. large diced fresh tomatoes
12 jumbo stuffed green olives

Season the breasts with salt and white pepper and dredge in flour. Shake off excess and sauté in clarified butter until golden brown. Remove onto a platter.

Remove all but one tablespoon of butter and sauté the onions for 2-3 minutes until brown all around. Add garlic. Sauté gently for 1/2 minute and add white wine, stock, bay leaf, thyme, and paste; and simmer until reduced by half. Make a roux by adding the 3 tablespoons of flour to the butter after it has melted; simmer the two together until the flour is light brown. Add it to the stock mixture and with a whip mix in completely. Sauté mushrooms and add them; simmer for five minutes more. Place chicken and olives in sauce; simmer five more minutes.

Place on plates, add tomatoes to sauce, toss gently, spoon sauce over breasts.

Stove Top Chicken with Scarlet Rice & Emerald Peas

Red rice is popular provender in South Carolina (sometimes it's even called Savannah Rice). In honor of Miss Katie Scarlett O'Hara, we dubbed this dish "Scarlet Rice." A visually beautiful dinner entree, the green peas add an oomph of color (plus an enticing extra nuance of flavor) to a happy medley of chicken, onions, etc.

* * *

1 1/2 c. canned tomatoes, chopped
1 1/2 c. water

1/4 tsp. salt
1 c. raw rice
1 c. onion, chopped
1 c. green pepper
4 pieces uncooked chicken (We like ours with the skin
    removed.)
2 c. green peas (fresh or frozen)
Texas Pete hot sauce to taste

Put the first seven ingredients into a large pot. Bring to
a boil. Lower heat and simmer until the chicken is tender
(about an hour). Just before serving stir in the peas and cook
only a few minutes more. Season with hot sauce, if desired.

Barbecue in Mr. Faulkner's Backyard

*Whenever I think of "barbecued anything," I
automatically have two mental associations: Johnny Harris
Barbecue in Savannah, and a flat tire in Oxford, Mississippi.
Why, you may wonder, a flat tire in Oxford, Mississippi? I'm
glad you asked!*

*One afternoon when Henry was still stationed in
Dayton, Ohio (but we had already fallen in love with New
Orleans), we were returning to Dayton from a trip to New
Orleans. A keg of spilled nails on I-55 in north Mississippi
stopped our Mustang in her tracks. After changing tires, we
exited the interstate and drove east to Oxford for a repair on
our damaged "horse shoe." Well, after some delays, we
decided just to spend the night in this newly-discovered and
delightful detour. The tree-studded campus enthralled us, as
did the relaxed, cozy ambience of the town. We ate barbecue
for supper, then enjoyed the caressingly warm and humid
evening eating Brown Mule popsicles and exploring the streets
of Oxford . . . .*

*Following are some of my best recipes for barbecue of
various types.*

Rhett Butler's Barbecued Chicken

Neither silly, fickle, nor simperingly sweet, Rhett Butler's Barbecued Chicken is suave, sophisticated, and fiery. Surely the holds of Capt. Butler's ships were packed with cases of Worcestershire sauce along with guns, ammunition, and the latest Parisian fashions!

The marinade for this chicken can be stirred up in advance and stored in the refrigerator. It will keep almost indefinitely. The recipe is enough to marinate at least two chickens. This variation of the classic Southern entree will win you a reputation as a skillful cook. — A dinnertime sensation!

* * *

1 c. dry sherry
3 tbsp. Worcestershire sauce
3 tbsp. lemon juice
2 tbsp. vegetable oil
2 tbsp. mayonnaise
2 1/2 tsp. black pepper
2 tsp. dry thyme
1 tsp. garlic powder
1 small onion, minced finely

Combine everything, then beat well. (I use a rotary egg beater.) Pour into a glass jar to store in the refrigerator. When you are ready to prepare Rhett Butler's Barbecued Chicken, place uncooked chicken pieces in a Pyrex baking dish. Beat marinade thoroughly and pour over chicken. (The sauce should be about half an inch deep in the dish.) Cover with plastic wrap, and put in the refrigerator for several hours or overnight.

Three hours before you wish to serve Rhett Butler's Barbecued Chicken, transfer the chicken pieces to a foil-lined pan and pour on the sauce in which the pieces have been marinating. Cover pan tightly with another sheet of aluminum foil, and put in a 300° F. oven. Bake for three hours.

The optimum accompaniment? Sweet potatoes, of course. — We're talking Southern!

Southside Barbecued Venison

If possible, this is even better than pork or beef barbecue! If you can get hold of some venison, by all means, fix this dish! (Where'd I get the name for this concoction? We live in the part of central Virginia known as the "Southside.")

* * *

4-5 c. cooked venison, shredded [Stew cubed venison three hours or until extremely tender. When cool, shred. (I use my fingers to shred it up.)]
3 c. liquid from stewing venison
2 c. canned tomato sauce
1/2 c. vinegar
2 tbsp. brown sugar, packed
1/2 c. onion, chopped
2 cloves garlic, minced
1 1/2 tsp. salt
1/2 tsp. cinnamon
1/4 tsp. cloves
Black and red pepper, and/or Tabasco to taste

Simmer together the above ingredients, covered, for an hour. Stir occasionally. Serve on warmed hamburger buns. (My whole wheat hamburger buns make it extra-good! See my *Well, Bless Your Heart, Vol. I* cookbook for a recipe.)

Limas or coleslaw are compatible accompaniments.

The Bucks Stopped Here

Let me digress here a moment to tell you about how I "got involved with" venison.

One day a Chatham friend of ours, Richard Motley, unexpectedly brought us the front leg of a deer he had killed. I had never cooked venison before (although we had eaten it, and love it!). He instructed us to cube up the meat for stew. We did so, and put it into the freezer. The next day at church

I asked another friend of ours, Butch Lawrence, how to prepare venison stew. We briefly discussed some different recipe ideas.

Well, lo and behold, the following afternoon what should appear on our front porch but two very large deer rumps, compliments of Butch and his wife Liz! The rumps were in large plastic garbage bags, one of which had split and was leaking blood all over the porch. When I discovered the deer meat (and blood) a photography customer was due to arrive any moment to pick up an order. I quickly pulled the dead-weight-heavy rumps inside (feeling a bit like Scarlett O'Hara dragging the corpse of the Yankee straggler she had just shot in the face) and got them up on the table. Rapid work with towels eliminated the evidence just in time for me to calmly greet the photography customer!

Subsequently I prepared magnificent barbecues, roasts, and stews from those, my first gift portions of deer. Here is an enticingly tasty venison stew for you:

The Buck Stops Here Stew

2-3 c. cubed cooked venison (stewed in advance for three
    hours or until tender)
2 c. cooking water from venison
2 large onions, chopped
2 potatoes, quartered
2 carrots, in thick slices
1/2 tsp. salt, or more to taste
1/2 tsp. dried parsley
1/2 tsp. dried thyme
1/2 tsp. dried marjoram
1/2 tsp. Texas Pete hot sauce
1/4 tsp. black pepper
1 clove garlic, minced
1 bay leaf
1/2 c. dry white or red wine

Combine all ingredients except wine. Cover and simmer 1 1/2 hours, stirring occasionally. For optimum blending of flavors, refrigerate overnight, and re-heat to serve. Before serving, remove bay leaf. Add wine and heat briefly (do not boil). Adjust seasonings if necessary, and serve. (We like grits as a side dish!)

Grits

To 4 cups of boiling water add 1 cup of grits and 1 tsp. salt. Bring to a boil. Reduce heat to medium. Cover and cook for 20-30 minutes. Stir often to prevent sticking. Add water to get desired consistency. Serve hot with butter. Serves 4.

- recipe courtesy Teague's Mill, Gatlinburg, TN

Cheese Grits Casserole

Cook grits as above (20 minutes). Put in buttered dish. Dot top with butter. Layer Swiss or any other cheese on top. Cover. Bake at 350° F. until the cheese melts.

- recipe courtesy Teague's Mill, Gatlinburg, TN

20th Century Roast Venison

1 1/2 lb. venison roast
Water to cover
1 rounded tbsp. salt
1 tsp. baking soda
1/2 c. vinegar

1/2 pkg. dry Lipton Onion Soup Mix
2 tbsp. vegetable oil
1 1/2 c. dry red or white wine
1/2 c. green pepper, chopped or in rings

The day before you want to serve roast venison, put the meat in a non-metal container. Barely cover with water. Add salt, soda, and vinegar. Cover and let soak, refrigerated, until the next day. Then drain off the liquid, and place the roast in the center of a large sheet of aluminum foil in a baking pan. Pull up the sides of the foil and add the four final ingredients. Fold together the edges of the foil to "lock in" the meat and juices. Bake at 375° F. for 2 1/2 - 3 hours or until fork-tender.

20th Century Roast Venison is absolutely *platonic* ("none better of its type")! I serve a seasonal raw vegetable salad in a separate course preceding this roast, and accompany the meat with F&P Skillet Scallop (see the recipe after the following one). Fresh fruit (grapes, for instance) makes a refreshing meal finale.

Roast Venison with Wine

7 1/2 lb. leg of venison roast
1 tbsp. vegetable oil
1/2 tsp. salt
1/4 tsp. black pepper
1/4 tsp. thyme
2 tbsp. onion, chopped
1 clove garlic, minced
1/4 c. lemon juice
1 c. broth from stewing other parts of your deer
      (or 1 c. beef bouillon)
1 c. red wine

Put two large sheets of aluminum foil on a baking pan. Place the meat in the center and raise up the edges. Mix the remaining ingredients together and pour over the venison. Fold together the edges of the foil, sealing tightly. Place in a 425° F. oven and cook 3 1/2 hours, or until extremely tender.

F&P Skillet Scallop

So easy, and *so* yummy! This potato dish is *fast* (and it fast became a Mitchell family favorite) and *perfect* with roasts, meat loaf, barbecued chicken, etc. Depending upon how thinly you slice the potatoes, this vegetable treasure can be ready in half an hour.

Incidentally, at the turn of the century the F&P (Franklin & Pittsylvania) Railroad connected our neighboring towns of Rocky Mount and Gretna, running on a very haphazard schedule. Its initials gave rise to a tongue-in-cheek designation, the *Fast & Perfect*. As the story goes, the train was chugging along near Sandy Level (home of the aforementioned Butch and Liz Lawrence) when it pulled alongside a farmer on foot. "Wanna ride?" — "Nope, I'd rather walk. I'm in a hurry." On its last run the F&P was documented as covering 8 miles in 8 hours!

* * *

1 tbsp. butter or margarine
4 potatoes, thinly sliced
2 medium onions, thinly sliced
1 c. milk
Salt, pepper, paprika to taste

Melt the butter or margarine in a skillet. Add the veggies, milk, and seasonings. Heat to boiling; reduce heat and simmer, covered, until the potatoes are tender. (I remove the lid a few minutes before serving, so that the liquid cooks down.)

Katie's Rice

Another exemplary side dish, Katie's Rice is often requested by Katie Peery. (Katie is the daughter of Henry's secretary, Faye.) Katie is obviously a young lady with a knowledgeable palate, for this is a gourmet treat!

1 stick butter, cut into four pieces
1 1/4 c. converted rice, uncooked
1 can cream of mushroom soup
1 can beef consommé soup
1 small jar mushrooms, drained
1 can water chestnuts (chopped and drained)
1 onion, chopped
1 green pepper, chopped
Salt and pepper to taste

Put butter into bottom of greased casserole dish. Add remaining ingredients and mix well. Cover. Bake for about 1 hour and 20 minutes at 325° F.

Carroll County Corn Casserole

My family and I were first served this satisfying food by Helen Melton of Hillsville, Virginia. (Helen is a "five-star" cook. I am indebted to her for many of my recipes!)

We had been traveling all day, and were tired and ravenous when we sat down to eat at the Melton's dining room table. (It was during those "magic days" between Christmas and New Year's, and Joe and Helen's house and table were as beautifully decorated as a Christmas shop.) Anyway, this Carroll County Corn Casserole, which is really more like a corn bread, tasted mighty welcome! I 'bout filled up on three servings of it (accompanied by beaucoups of flavorful pintos). — I also managed to eat plenty of mashed potatoes, some string beans, a slice of country ham, a bit of cranberry salad soufflé, a roll, several of Helen's four different kinds of homemade pickle (she makes others, too, but Icicle, Bread & Butter, Dill, and Pickled Beets were presented at this meal), and then Apricot Fluff for dessert!! My, My! — Do try Carroll County (location of Hillsville) Corn Casserole . . . .

* * *

1/2 stick butter or margarine, melted
1 can (1 lb.) creamed corn
1/2 small box Jiffy corn muffin mix (or enough self-rising
    corn meal to form a moderately stiff batter)
1 egg, beaten
1 c. sour cream

      Combine all ingredients. Bake in 1 1/2 - quart baking
dish at 350° F. for 45 minutes.

'Bama Burger Casserole

      When we moved to New Orleans we first lived at 823
Ursuline Street in the Quarter. (Later we moved to 612
Royal.) Because we just wanted to be there, and were not on
any particular "career tracks" we did whatever (honest-type)
jobs we found. First I worked as a stock clerk at Walgreen's
on Royal Street, and Henry operated a carriageway art
gallery. Later on I managed a gift shop, and he sold antiques
at Morton's. Occasionally we held down several different
jobs at once! For awhile we operated Robert's Hideaway, a
small restaurant on the courtyard at 612 Royal Street. (The
restaurant was owned by Robert Bernissant.)

      As part of our wages, we got to eat lunch and dinner
free of charge. Boy, did we dish up the Shrimp Creole, both
for customers and ourselves!! — Not to mention the number
of chocolate éclairs we consumed!

      Eventually we bought the Cajun Queen Gift Shop at
which I had been working and renamed it "Mitchells." We
stocked locally handcrafted items such as Madame Chapeaux
Dolls; Jack Miller and Phillip Sage etchings; and Soren
Pederson's jewelry. Business was brisk, and Henry came on
board to help. — We soon started publishing a French Quarter
magazine called *The Community Standard*.

      But, hold on, you don't want to read an autobiography,
you want to cook! The following is an easy-to-fix casserole,
recipe compliments of my friend, Jane Cox, lovely belle from

Alabama. — (One night when I had to work late at Walgreen's, I had prepared this recipe and Henry ate *THE WHOLE THING!)*

* * *

1 1/2 lb. ground beef
1 medium onion, chopped
1/2 c. green pepper, chopped
1 can cream of mushroom soup
1 can cream of chicken soup
1 can niblet corn with pimiento
3 c. egg noodles, cooked
1 c. sour cream
Salt and pepper

Brown meat, onion, and green pepper. Drain. Cook noodles. Combine everything and pour into a large casserole dish. Bake at 350° F. for 45 minutes. Serves six or eight.

Note: "Mock" sour cream can be made by blending 1 c. cottage cheese and 1 tbsp. lemon juice in a blender until smooth. This is more nutritious than regular sour cream, adding protein rather than fat to a dish.

Barbecued Shrimp à la Mary Grey

During our New Orleans days, we found that our lives were somewhat intertwined with those of Doug and Mary Grey Hardwick. We had business ties and interacted socially. They also witnessed to us about the new life in Christ (seemingly with no effect, but seeds were planted which later grew and blossomed into two born-again lives). — One night for dinner at their house, Mary Grey served this incomparable New Orleans specialty.

* * *

1 lb. butter
1 tsp. each salt, paprika, and black pepper
Juice of 1/2 lemon
2 tsp. finely-minced garlic

2 crushed bay leaves
1/2 tsp. each basil, oregano, rosemary, and cayenne pepper
2 lbs. whole fresh shrimp in the shell, washed

In a heavy saucepan melt the butter. Add the seasonings, and stir until the mixture comes to a slow boil.

Pour over the unpeeled shrimp which have been spread in a large pan (9 1/2 x 11 is a good size).

Put under the broiler for three to four minutes or until the sauce is bubbly and the shrimp are cooked. (If you like the shrimp crispy, turn them once and run them back under the broiler for one minute.)

Note: Be sure to serve Barbecued Shrimp with plenty of French bread to dip into the highly-seasoned butter sauce. — In New Orleans, folks eat the shrimp shells, antennae, and all. If you feel more fastidious than that, you may peel them. At Pascal's Manale Restaurant on Napoleon Avenue in New Orleans, literally tons of these peppery shrimp go "down the hatch." — Incidentally, for home-cooked Barbecued Shrimp in New Orleans (or places that sell the about-to-be-mentioned product), there is a short cut: Buy a box of Zatarain's Crab Boil, dump it into a pound of melted butter, and *voilà, you are ready to broil your shrimp.*

How Many Shrimp Was That?

Incidentally, speaking of shrimp, Hubby tells a cute story about his mother's learning to serve shrimp. John, Henry's older brother, was dating his wife-to-be, a petite Savannah beauty. His enthusiasm for her and coastal cuisine caused mom Mary to prepare shrimp for the first time. Henry recalls her offering the average-sized fried shrimp with the question, "Do you want one or two?"

Now John is married to a lovely Annapolis lady who makes out-of-this-world crab cakes! It's amazing what gourmet delights can grow on one's family tree!

Delights in the New Orleans Night

New Orleans is a city of enchantment. Like the surprise of glimpsing a rainbow in the spray from a riverboat's paddlewheel, the city's charms can pounce upon you suddenly — a whiff of sweet olive as you stroll past St. Anthony's Garden to the rear of the St. Louis Cathedral — or they can be anticipated — the magic of a streetcar ride at dusk, or the lingering balminess of an evening spent on the patio at Pat O'Brien's. Other nights to remember in New Orleans include, for me, a wild tour of the city from the rear of a motorcycle; late-night swims at the Olivier Guest House and Downtowner Burgundy swimming pools; long ambles around the Quarter; conversations with friends about life and afterlife until 4 AM; slow revolutions in the Top of the Mart watching Canal Street and then the River; the surfeit of joy, "blues," and stimulation afforded by the music at Preservation Hall. And, of course, there are the evening meals — often a day's high point. Anyone can get lyrical about New Orleans food! A dinner of gumbo, pompano, French bread, and caramel cup custard, or other typical stellar combinations will have you raving, too. (Even the humble red beans and rice make you appreciative!) Later on, beignets might culminate a night of delight in The City That Care Forgot. . . .

The three following recipes are fit for the fork of a seasoned Louisianian.

Choice Saucy Seafood

This seafood extravaganza is truly magnificent — the shrimp, scallops, chunks of crabmeat and lobster look irresistible in the rich cheese sauce.

* * *

1/4 c. butter or margarine
2 3/4 c. celery, chopped
2 c. onions, chopped
1/2 c. butter or margarine
1/2 tsp. salt
1/4 tsp. black pepper

3/4 c. all-purpose flour
2 1/2 c. milk
2 c. Cheddar cheese, grated
5-6 c. of a combination (as you like) of cooked seafoods —
lobster, crab, shrimp, scallops, tuna, etc.)

In a skillet, sauté the celery and onions in the 1/4 c. butter until tender; season. In a saucepan melt the 1/2 c. butter; stir in the flour, blending it in completely. Slowly add the milk, stirring to form a thickened sauce. Stir in the cheese. — Remove from heat.

Combine celery/onion mixture with the cooked seafoods; spoon into one large casserole dish (or 6 to 8 individual ramekins). Pour the sauce over the seafood combination. Bake at 350° F. for 15-20 minutes or until bubbly and brown.

Old Glory Wins Again

When Henry and I operated a restaurant in the French Quarter of New Orleans, we learned to truly appreciate individuals in the food service industry. — Serving the public is not always easy!

One night I particularly remember. It was a sauna-warm and moist New Orleans twilight. Our little courtyard, with its bevy of votive-candle-lit wrought iron tables, was busy with couples and groups dining. At one table sat a Canadian family. The man and woman had succumbed to the romance of the Vieux Carré and were immersed in each other, leaving their young son to amuse himself (as they lingered over dessert and each other). The little boy had evidently purchased earlier a package of decals of the American flag. To amuse himself the lad (unbeknownst to us at the time), was sticking those flags on the glasses, the cups, the dishes, the glass top of the table, even the dinnerware. — Henry and I discovered that these stickers were virtually impossible to remove! At well past midnight we were still scrubbing gummy mess off wine glasses and plates. Oh, well, as I mentioned, we did learn that waiters, waitresses, and others on the staffs of restaurants must be gracious, even in patience-trying circumstances!

Fillet Mornay

Very "Frenchy" in flavor, but sublimely easy to prepare, Fillet Mornay is a Mitchell house specialty (even the kids love it!). This entree has a subtle, smooth taste and texture; and, like a majority of my most-used recipes, it utilizes standard ingredients — no pine nuts, capers, or caviar!

As they say in Louisiana, "First you make a roux . . . ." That's the fat and flour mixture which is heated to form the basis of this simple Mornay Sauce. (A roux, you know, is the starting point of many sauces and soups.) Once you've made the sauce, the oven does the rest!

* * *

1 lb. fish fillets (perch, trout, what have you — you choose),
    thawed if frozen
2 tbsp. vegetable oil
3 tbsp. flour
1/4 tsp. salt
Dash of pepper
1 1/2 c. milk
3 tbsp. Parmesan cheese
Paprika

Place the fish in a baking dish. Meanwhile, heat the oil slightly and blend in the flour. Add salt and pepper. Cook briefly, stirring constantly. Gradually add the milk, beating to remove all lumps. When the sauce is thickened, fold in Parmesan cheese. Pour this sauce over the fillets, and sprinkle with paprika. Bake covered at 375° F. for 15 minutes; then remove cover and bake 15 minutes more, or until the fish flakes easily with a fork. Serves 4.

Unexcelled Seafood Casserole

Enough for a crowd, this delectable casserole is ideal for a buffet.
* * *

2 tbsp. butter or margarine
1 onion, finely chopped
1 c. celery, finely chopped
1 green pepper, chopped
2 (4-oz.) cans mushrooms, drained
2 c. wild rice, cooked
2 c. white rice, cooked
2 cans cream of mushroom soup
1 (16-oz.) can bean sprouts, drained
2 c. crabmeat, cooked (canned is O. K.)
2 c. shrimp, cooked
Salt and pepper to taste
1 c. buttered bread crumbs
1 c. Cheddar or American cheese, grated

Sauté the onion, celery, peppers, and mushrooms in butter. Then mix with rice (the two types of which have been cooked separately), soup, sprouts, seafood, salt, and pepper. Spoon into a greased 2-quart baking dish. Sprinkle with crumbs and cheese. Bake in the baking dish while it sits in a large pan of water, at 350° F. for 40 minutes.

Avery Island Barbecued Chicken

Named for Louisiana's fabled Avery Island, reknowned for its Tabasco sauce, its bird sanctuary and gardens, this recipe produces a non-tomatoey type of barbecue sauce. Simple and tasty!

* * *

1/2 c. prepared mustard
1/2 c. molasses
1/2 c. vinegar
1/2 tsp. Tabasco
4-5 pieces uncooked chicken

Combine the first four ingredients. Meanwhile, place the chicken pieces in a foil-lined pan. Pour over the sauce and bake uncovered at 375° F. for an hour and 15 minutes, basting occasionally. If the chicken gets too brown, cover with foil. If it gets too dry, add a small amount of water.

Louisiana Chicken Pot

Pretend you are a Cajun and cook up this "big pot" dish — they'd use a lot more cayenne pepper, though!

* * *

1 1/2 tbsp. vegetable oil
1 heaping tbsp. flour
2 1/4 c. onion, chopped
1 1/4 c. green (bell) pepper, chopped
3 cloves garlic, minced
1/4 - 1/2 tsp. salt
1/2 tsp. thyme
1/4 tsp. black pepper
1/8 - 1/4 tsp. cayenne pepper
1 1/2 tsp. Worcestershire sauce
4-5 pieces uncooked chicken
3 c. canned tomatoes, undrained and chopped

Combine the oil and flour in a large pot. Cook together, stirring almost continuously until the "roux" is golden brown. Add onions, green bell pepper, and garlic, stir, and cover. Let cook a few minutes, stirring occasionally. Add the remaining ingredients, stir, and partially cover. Let cook until the chicken is tender, about an hour. Stir often during the cooking period. Serve over rice.

Squeeze on the Orange, Tug on the Heartstrings

You might wonder, if you have read my other books and know about our fondness for New Orleans, why we ever moved away from there. You know we love New Orleans food, people, climate, architecture, etc., but we left there for want of an orange juice squeezer. — To expound on that point: after I broke a small bone in the side of my foot, we became more conscious of the value of proper nutrition (calcium, vitamin C, and so forth). We went on "a health food kick," and I began preparing more natural whole foods. I wanted freshly-squeezed orange juice, and a cursory search of French Quarter shops yielded no old-fashioned glass container with a "fluted hump" in the center and a "moat" around it.

That lack, plus inconvenient renovation of our building, caused us to think longingly of home — family ties and a simpler, rural Virginia lifestyle, complete with gadgets from the good old days. The failed search for an orange-juice squeezer became symbolic of a void in our lives we felt could better be remedied "back home."

Soon we divested ourselves of our business and set our moving date. Friends came by to bid us adieu. On the morning we were leaving one friend, Soren Pederson, came to our apartment. He had heard "what set us off," and had found an orange juice squeezer for us! — This touching act brought tears to our eyes, but the rented station wagon was already packed.

Reminiscences of Virginia

Henry and I both grew up here in Southside Virginia, he in the small community of Spring Garden, I in little Dry Fork. My memories of summer nights are joyous — watching the sun set over the nearby field of (on alternating years) corn or tobacco, as flocks of sleepily chirping birds perched on the electric wires; chasing lightning bugs; playing with visiting cousins. (Winter nights seem to have been endless evenings of tedious torture, sitting at my desk, laboring over my math books . . . .)

Henry remembers the fun of sitting in his yard and watching flying squirrels. (We had no squirrel-appealing trees, so I have yet to see a flying squirrel.) — Henry states that he just liked to be outside at night, to smell the night air, and listen to the cicadas. His sister Joan fondly remembers sitting on the front porch on a summer night and watching a cedar tree silhouetted against the rising moon. Later the children walked up to the end of the front sidewalk and identified the constellations.

Brother John remembers the exhilaration of driving home late at night on the "Snake Path" (the winding road between Dry Fork and Spring Garden), and dipping down into

Sweeting Fork Creek valley. A rush of cooler, moist, honeysuckle-scented air greeted one there through the open car windows . . . .

Henry's most vivid memory of deluxe Dixie dinners involves leisurely evenings spent at the dining room table of his mother's cousins, Paul and Flossie Hash of Starkey (near Roanoke), Virginia. Their home boasted many giant ancient boxwoods, a kitchen with a fireplace tall enough to stand up in, and — just off the kitchen, through a door — a spring-house room with constantly-running cold mountain water. In the parlor, amongst the antique furniture and Oriental rugs, was a grand piano (the Hashes were both musicians), and in the yard was a flock of ducks — one of which was often called upon to make the Supreme Sacrifice for duck dinner with all the trimmings. The Hashes, childless and therefore less modestly practical than most of Henry's family, spared no details in serving, with all the china, silver, crystal, and linen one could want. "As a child, this was my first clue that dining could be more Roman than Spartan," Henry comments.

Faye O. Peery Spinach Lasagna

Speaking of "foreign," the name of this Italian dish has an Irish sound to it (as in Faye O'Peery), but actually Faye Oakes Peery is not much Irish. What she is, is an excellent secretary (to Henry at the planetarium), and a capable cook for her husband G. W. and their daughter Katie. Faye is so efficient and organized, like many working women, that she can toil eight hours in an office, and then go home and prepare a dinner of which to be proud. This main dish really is a meal-in-itself, because it contains protein, starch (the pasta), and even the vegetables — spinach and carrots.

While on the topic of spinach, let me tell you a funny story about a newlywed, a pressure cooker, and a "bad day." One evening my Dad came home to find his new little bride (this was before I came along, obviously!) sitting in a kitchen chair crying as though her heart would break. Imagining death and disaster, my Daddy inquired as to the cause of the waterworks. Without even looking up, Mom pointed to the ceiling. Had someone gone to heaven? Dad raised his eyes to behold — spinach plastered to the top of the room! The pressure cooker had erupted.

Never fear, in this recipe you don't face the challenge of cooking spinach "under pressure!"

* * *

1 1/2 - oz. pkg. spaghetti sauce mix
1 (6-oz.) can tomato paste with garlic
1 (15 1/2 - oz.) can tomato sauce
1 tsp. sugar
1 tsp. basil
2 1/2 c. water
2 eggs, beaten
1 (16-oz.) carton ricotta cheese
1 (10-oz.) pkg. frozen chopped spinach, thawed and drained
1 1/2 c. grated carrots
1/2 c. grated Parmesan cheese, divided
1/2 (16-oz.) pkg. lasagna noodles
2 (6-oz.) pkg. mozzarella slices

Combine spaghetti sauce mix, tomato paste, tomato sauce, sugar, basil, and water in a saucepan. Bring to a boil over medium heat. Remove and set aside.

Combine eggs, ricotta cheese, spinach, carrots, and 1/4 c. Parmesan cheese. Stir well. Set aside.

Spread 1 c. of the tomato mixture in a lightly-greased 13x9x2-inch baking dish. Layer half of the *uncooked* lasagna noodles, spinach and carrot mixture, mozzarella cheese, and tomato mixture. Repeat layers. Sprinkle remaining Parmesan cheese on top.

Cover tightly with aluminum foil and bake at 350° F. for 1 hour. After removing from the oven, let the lasagna stand 10 minutes before serving.

Not Far from Home

One of our fun places to go is nearby Greensboro, North Carolina, a small city well-supplied with commendable restaurants. (Near Greensboro is the picturesque Old Mill of Guilford, site of many jaunts to purchase wholegrain flours.) One of the superb restaurants in Greensboro is Amalfi Harbor. Chefs Robert and Angela Martin were kind enough to share the next recipes with me for your enjoyment.

Shrimp (Scampi) Amalfi

Ingredients per portion:

8 butterflied shrimp (tail and last joint on)
1 oz. melted butter
1 oz. oil
1 oz. chicken stock
1 oz. Marsala wine or any white wine
1 tbsp. fresh chopped garlic or more

Mix all in a small saucepan. Cook shrimp 3 minutes on each side or until cooked. Garnish with parsley and lemon wedges.

Shrimp with Spanish Sauce

Ingredients per four portions:

32 butterflied shrimp (tail and last joint on)
6 oz. tomato sauce
1/4 yellow onion, sliced thinly
1/2 of green pepper, sliced thinly
2 fresh okra, sliced
2 or 3 mushrooms, sliced thinly
Celery, sliced thinly
1/2 of red pepper, sliced thinly
Salt and pepper to taste
Fresh garlic

Cook all in saucepan until vegetables are tender. Add raw shrimp and cook 5 minutes. Serve over cooked rice or noodles.

It's a Date

My parents worked at Hargrave Military Academy in Chatham as I was growing up. (In fact, Dad was there 35 years.) In theory, this gave me, as a budding teenager, easy access to potential "date material." Probably some of my female peers envied the fact that I frequently attended athletic events on campus and that we ate many meals in the school dining hall. If any boys did interest me, though, my nearsighted eyes could seldom spot them as they marched into the dining room in their identical gray uniforms. To me the human columns were gray seas of 300 crew cuts. However, as I grew older, I figured that some of the lads at nearby tables (the faculty sat at separate tables) might be observing me, so I attempted to eat daintily, not gorging on the fried chicken and mashed potatoes (Sunday dinner menu) or the franks and sauerkraut (weeknight fare). Actually, the only indication of student interest in me was the fact that when the ubiquitous blocks of oft-served ice cream appeared on our table, a neighboring student table was quick to offer to trade flavors when we received strawberry. (I preferred chocolate, Neapolitan, or vanilla.)

Proper table manners and ladylikeness perhaps helped because I did date a few Hargrave boys, but God was growing up the perfect mate for me over in Spring Garden. Soon Henry came on the scene, and gray-clad cadets were all superseded. Before long we eloped to Raleigh, North Carolina!

Associated with thoughts of ice cream, what Southern dinner would be complete without dessert (or sometimes in the South that would be plural — DESSERTS!)? Here is a pie classic from our dating days. Henry's mom served this often when we came home to Pittsylvania County from Virginia Tech. On our first visit after eloping, Mary again prepared this favorite of ours with "wedding cake" bride and groom figures on top!

Goin' Courtin' Lemon Meringue Pie

1 baked pie shell
7 tbsp. cornstarch

1 1/2 c. sugar
1/2 tsp. salt
2 c. boiling water
3 eggs, separated
1/4 c. fresh lemon juice
2 tbsp. butter or margarine
2 tbsp. grated lemon peel

Combine the cornstarch, sugar, and salt in a double boiler pot. Add the water. Stir constantly, until thick. Cover and place over boiling water. Cook for 10 minutes, stirring occasionally. Beat the egg yolks slightly; add a little of the hot mixture; stir and pour the egg mixture into the pot. Cook 2 minutes, stirring the entire time. Remove from the heat, and stir in lemon juice, butter, and lemon peel. Cool to room temperature without stirring. Pour into a cooled baked pastry shell.

Next, prepare the meringue this way: add 1 tsp. lemon juice to the 3 egg whites. Beat with an electric mixer until it's stiff enough to hold peaks. Sprinkle in 6 tbsp. sugar, one at a time, beating after each addition. Pile meringue lightly on the pie. Bake at 350° F. for 15 or 20 minutes to lightly brown the meringue. Cool before serving.

Music of the Beach

The thought of desserts "puts me in mind of" the desserts at our beach "retreat," the Chesterfield Inn in Myrtle Beach, South Carolina. When Phillip or Marvin rattle off the list of dessert choices after a huge and scrumptious dinner in the charming old oceanfront dining room, it's hard to decide which treat to select! After a repast of appetizer, salad, perhaps flounder or shrimp or prime rib, vegetables, and biscuits, plus dessert, a bit of exercise is certainly in order!

Reminisce with me . . . . Nights in Myrtle Beach mean for some people boozing and cruising, but since my childhood, an evening there consists of a button-poppingly-bountiful meal at the Chesterfield or another restaurant, and then a walk to the Pavilion amusement park. I've never liked the scary rides, but even before antique carousels were "in vogue" I loved the Herschell-Spillman work of art "merry-go-round" at the Pavilion. Even now I revel in riding on the menagerie fantasy, supposedly helping to steady one of our young children as they experience the ups and downs of a bright green giant frog or a bejeweled swine or a running, teeth-bared tiger, or, of course, a majestic horse.

When the creatures stop spinning, we saunter around, pausing to look at the 1900 German pipe organ (over 400 pipes, 98 keys, and in the style of a grand circus wagon). The kids ride a few more rides. Then it's across the street to the trick mirrors, and the Gay Dolphin Gift Shop. (When you've been doing something for decades, you don't easily change your pattern . . . .)

To draw the curtain on the carnival atmosphere, we walk along the beach, back to the our hotel. The midnight blue sky and ocean seem to merge into a velvet drapery, studded with rhinestones above and trimmed at the bottom in fluttery lace. An occasional leaning palmetto lends a tropical feeling to the warm, salt-spray-perfumed night. It's romantic, it's awesome, it's a whole lot to be thankful for!

Now for some more dessert recipes to gladden your heart . . . .

Southern Nights Homemade Ice Cream

Believe it or not, even after the Chesterfield's evening feast, we sometimes cannot resist stopping at a booth at the Pavilion to select ice cream cones with flavored crusty toppings. Even more memorable, though, are the summer-evening Sunday-school-class picnics of a few years back at Rick and Mott Cline's cabin on the wooded bank of Cherrystone Lake near Chatham. While the charcoal heated up for grilling hot dogs and hamburgers, the menfolk took turns cranking the ice cream freezers. Canisters of vanilla and chocolate ice cream were produced, but the group's favorite was peach, made with peaches freshly picked at a nearby orchard.

After thus fully developing our taste for homemade ice cream, you can imagine our delight in obtaining Faye Peery's "best-of-the-best" recipe.

* * *

8 eggs
2 c. sugar
2 tbsp. vanilla
1 pt. whipping cream
4 cans Eagle brand condensed milk
3 quarts milk

Combine eggs, cream, sugar, and vanilla in a bowl. Mix thoroughly. Add condensed milk and regular milk. For fruit cream, add 2 1/2 cups of peaches, bananas, strawberries, etc. Refrigerate before freezing — overnight if possible, but at least long enough to cool all the ingredients. Then proceed according to the instructions of your ice cream freezer's manufacturer. This recipe makes 2 gallons (when fruit is used).

Dare you bake Faye's Pecan Pie, slices of which to place under her ice cream?!

Faye Peery's Pecan Pie

3 eggs, beaten
1/2 c. sugar
1 c. Karo - white
1/8 tsp. salt
1/4 c. butter, melted
1 tsp. vanilla
1 c. pecans, crushed
1 unbaked pie shell

Combine the first six ingredients and beat well. Put the pecans into the pie shell. Slowly and gently pour the pie filling over the nuts. Bake at 350° F. 55-60 minutes.

Never Fail Pie Crust:

3 c. flour
Dash of salt
1 1/2 c. shortening
1 egg, well beaten
6 tbsp. water
2 tbsp. vinegar

Mix together flour, salt, and shortening. In a separate container add the water and vinegar to the well-beaten egg. Combine the two mixtures; chill. Divide the dough into three parts and roll out. Makes three pie shells.

Tout de Suite Cookies

If company shows up unexpectedly (which you can *expect* in the South!), or if the Cookie Monster suddenly assaults you or one of the other "significant individuals" in your life, *Tout de Suite* Cookies are an immediate solution to your sticky situation: "*TOOT SWEET*," you can satisfy a sweet tooth. (You can prepare these cookies in 15 minutes, then chill briefly.)

* * *

1/4 c. sugar
2 tbsp. vegetable oil
1/4 c. carob powder
1/2 c. milk
1/2 c. peanut butter
1 tsp. vanilla
2 c. quick oats

In a saucepan, combine the first four ingredients. Bring to a boil and boil one minute. Remove from heat and stir in the remaining ingredients. Using a spoon and your fingers form a dozen or so balls, flatten, and place on a plate. Cover with plastic wrap, chill, and serve.

Credit for all the following recipes goes to Helen Melton of Hillsville, Virginia, my "Dessert-Maker-Par-Excellence" friend!

Banana Supreme Pie

Helen's great-aunt Carrie Alley shared this recipe with Helen, and now with Helen's permission, I'm "revealing it to the world!"

* * *

1 can Eagle brand sweetened condensed milk
2 1/2 or 3 bananas (ripe, but firm)
1 c. pecans, chopped
1 (10-oz.) container Cool Whip topping
2 small pie crusts, or one large one

Boil milk (unopened, in can) in water for 4 hours, and cool overnight or for several hours. [Do not set can directly on burner!]

Bake crusts and let cool.

Open milk and put in bowl. (It is rather sweet and thick after boiling — like caramel.) Add one tablespoon Cool Whip to milk and stir to thin down. Add pecans to milk/Cool Whip mixture. Slice bananas into crusts; then add half the milk mixture to each crust and smooth over to cover bananas. Top with Cool Whip and chill until ready to serve.

Note: If you think you will use more than two pies, you may boil two or three cans of milk at once and store them in the refrigerator. The milk will keep several weeks after it is boiled and cooled.

Evangeline Peach Pie

We named this pie for our daughter Sarah Evangeline because the first food (and almost *only* food for a long time) that she would eat was canned peaches. (In restaurants sometimes she'd settle for lots of catsup on white bread. Nothing else appealed to her 1 1/2 - year - old taste buds.) Now, believe it or not, she eats almost anything, and has a talent for cooking and evaluating recipes on which I'm working!

This recipe was originally given to Helen Melton by her friend Mava Vass. The crumb topping makes it special and different. (Perhaps we should call it Mava's Marvelous Peach Pie!)

* * *

1 9-inch unbaked pie shell
1 c. sugar
1/4 c. all-purpose flour
1/8 tsp. nutmeg
1/2 c. butter or margarine
6 to 8 large ripe fresh peaches, peeled and quartered

Mix sugar, flour, and nutmeg. Cut in butter until crumbly. Sprinkle half the crumb mixture into the pie shell. Arrange peaches over the crumb mixture, and then sprinkle on remaining crumbs. Bake at 450° F. for 10 minutes, then at 350° F. for 30 minutes.

Kentucky Pound Cake

This is another recipe Helen "inherited" from Carrie Alley. — If you like your pound cake accompanied by pickles (as many do), you most assuredly must be Southern (or pregnant, or both!).

* * *

2 c. granulated sugar
2 1/2 c. self-rising flour
4 egg yolks
2 tbsp. *HOT* water
1 1/4 c. vegetable oil
1/2 tsp. nutmeg

1/2 tsp. cinnamon
1 c. crushed pineapple and juice
    (or one 8-oz. can crushed pineapple w/juice)
1 c. chopped pecans
4 egg whites

   Mix flour (sifted), and sugar, egg yolks, vegetable oil, hot water, spices, nuts, and pineapple (plus juice) in mixer. Beat egg whites until stiff and fold into above mixture. Bake in a 10-inch greased and floured tube pan at 350° F. for one hour. Test to see if done. Turn out on a cake rack to cool.

None Better

We have been privileged to dine on the ultimate in minestrone and perfectly sauced pastas in Rome, and then stroll on the Via Veneto. We've enjoyed elegant terrines, fois gras, escargots, and sorbets in Paris, followed by the sight of Notre Dame Cathedral at dusk. We have sat at tables at the foot of the Acropolis and eaten moussaka, squid, peasant salad (Greek Salad to Americans), and baklava. On Bay Street in Nassau we have feasted on conch fritters and grouper while admiring cruise ships in the harbor. In the aristocratic elegance of the London Ritz we had tea and all the "proper" accompaniments.

But, I declare, I do believe that the sun (and the moon) shine brighter on a certain fish camp on the Pearl River in Mississippi where we've had, among other things, mighty fine shrimp tails; on the Battery in Charleston after a supper begun with She-Crab Soup; on the dock in Beaufort, North Carolina, after a meal centered around fresh scallops; and on a particular eatery in the Smoky Mountains where one can fish for trout and then sit down to eat the same, just caught.

In other words, there's no place in the world quite as delightful as Dixie for dining and dreaming, living and loving!